BAY OF FLAGS
& OTHER POEMS

To Mick

for tony [moon

Dublin
2010

First published in 2010 by
Dedalus Press
13 Moyclare Road
Baldoyle
Dublin 13
Ireland

www.dedaluspress.com

ISBN 978 1 906614 24 9 (hardbound)
ISBN 978 1 906614 23 2 (paperback)

Dedalus Press titles are represented in North America
by Syracuse University Press, Inc., 621 Skytop Road,
Suite 110, Syracuse, New York 13244, and in the UK by
Central Books, 99 Wallis Road, London E9 5LN

Cover image, 'Crossover' © Terry Winters, 2007,
Oil on linen, 196 x 150 cm, Courtesy Matthew Marks Gallery, New York;
by permission of the artist

Dedalus Press receives financial assistant from
The Arts Council / An Chomhairle Ealaíon

BAY OF FLAGS
& OTHER POEMS

Enrique Juncosa

Translated from the Spanish by
Michael Smith

DEDALUS PRESS
DUBLIN, IRELAND

Contents

BAHÍA DE LAS BANDERAS / BAY OF FLAGS (2007)

6

For Victor Esposito

Prologue

The poems of Enrique Juncosa bear the stamp of the man, of his personality, his interests both professional and private. There is the assurance of the well-travelled man, a boundless curiosity about other peoples and places, an astonishingly broad interest in most of the major art forms, and an enthusiasm to experiment that matches the novelty of what he has encountered on his travels. What I find most striking, however, is his painterly eye, which is not surprising since his career has been as a distinguished art gallery director for many years.

> Flowers sunk in mud
> draw paths in the forest
> for furtive arsonist feet.
>
> Kingfisher and orchids
> are unusually frequent here.
> ('Reef by Night')
>
> The full moon
> disappears
> during a freezing night
> in Minnesota
> erasing its reflection
> on water.
> ('Eclipse')

This characteristic calls to mind the poetry of the Irish poet, Thomas McGreevy, also a distinguished director of an art gallery.

The hillsides were of rushing, silvered water,
Down,
And around,
And all across,
And about the white, gleaming tree-trunks,
Far as sensitive eyesight could see,
On both sides of the valley,
And beyond,
Everywhere,
The silvered swirling water!
                    ('Gioconda')

But this is not imagism although, doubtless, MacGreevy, through his friendship with Richard Aldington and other so-called imagists, was well aware of imagism and was influenced by it. Enrique Juncosa, however, is neither an imagist not a moralising poet. Above all else, I think he is a cosmopolitan poet, nationalistically rootless despite his Mallorcan birth and upbringing. He has thrown himself open-mindedly on the world at large, willing to confront whatever comes along, his eyes peeled to observe the odd and bizarre, and rejoicing in the sheer variety of humanity and its idiosyncrasies, from the United States to India and other far-flung places.

Some readers, biased against any kind of global or international allusions, may think that this cosmopolitanism is something shallow, by its very nature, a kind of picture-postcard kind of poetry. But although his poems may not be rooted in Juncosa's Mallorcan background, they are nonetheless rooted in his own personal life. And he is extremely frank about this. He is not afraid to tell us what he thinks and feels as he confronts the oddities of life. While there is especially, as I've said, a painterly quality to his work, there is also a cinematic quality. The influence of the techniques of modern painting and of modern cinematography have had a huge input into his poetry. Collage and fragmentation, cuts and jumps, an avoidance of narrative. The poems present us with scenes and situations, observations of exotic rituals, strange human behaviour; and they leave us to make up our own mind about what to think of all of this, how to respond. There is no tidying up of things, no end-of-poem moralising, no nostalgia. He is a poet of the non-local. And with so much poetry today being written as what Geoffrey

Hill memorably described as 'home-video poetry', this is something to be welcomed.

Ultimately, the poems are celebratory, of the world in all its incomprehensible strangeness and its beauty.

It is a tight, compact poetry even when Juncosa indulges his predilection for long lists of names, of people and places. This is a kind of shorthand. The names are of people and places that have engaged his attention and who have meant something to him. It's not simply name-dropping. It's the kind of allusiveness that one finds, for example, in Borges. These names and places are signposts to where he has been, and are intended to tell us something about himself and how he sees the world. And there is a lot of love in this and a sharp intelligence, but without pretense or cynicism.

Juncosa writes in free verse (it is impossible to imagine him writing in any other form). But like a good painter with his materials. he is extremely carefully in his use of language. The poems are void of verbosity, pared down to minimal deployment.

> To wake up
> in Patagonia:
> the ostriches
> drinking
> under the poplars.
>
> The dog toys
> with a dead armadillo,
> while ducks and ibises
> flutter
> over ponds.
>   ('Chacra Paradiso')

Juncosa's poetry has already achieved considerable recognition in Spain. This collection of his poems should extend that deserved recognition into the anglophone world.

Michael Smith
Dublin, 2009

LAS ESPIRALES NARANJA (2002)

ORANGE SPIRALS (2002)

El hospital efímero

*"No espero a nadie
e insisto que alguien tiene que llegar".*
—José Lezama Lima

Ephemeral Hospital

*"I am waiting for no one
and I insist someone must arrive."*
—José Lezama Lima

Autorretrato con 38 años

No quiero describir
ni mi rostro ni mi cuerpo.

He leído, he viajado y he sentido.

Pienso a menudo en Apollinaire en París,
o en Frank O'Hara en Nueva York...

Sin embargo no tengo casa
más allá de los bares del mundo.

Self-Portrait at 38

I have no wish to describe
either my body or my face.

I have read, I have travelled and I have felt.

I often think about Apollinaire in Paris,
or Frank O'Hara in New York ...

Yet I have no home
beyond the bars of the world.

La costa del oro

para Malcolm Morley

De Accrá a Dixcove
se suceden
fortalezas europeas
de cuatro siglos de antigüedad.

Se asemejan al refugio de los piratas
de Stevenson:
blanco desconchado y cañones herrumbrosos.

Elmina es una excepción
majestuosa
que nos lleva a inventar
en ensoñación tropical
refinados mercaderes portugueses
rendidos ante joyas de oro
Ashanti
y filigranas de marfil.
Catalejos que otean el horizonte
desde torreones fabulosos.

Pero Elmina son también mazmorras
terribles,
cementerios de esclavos
y vergüenza de Europa.
La morada de los murciélagos,
ahora,
como objetivación de un ritual animista.

Vudu mon amour.

The Gold Coast

for Malcolm Morley

From Accra to Dixcove
one can find
European fortresses
four centuries old.

They resemble the haven
of Stevenson's pirates:
dull white and rusty cannons.

Elmina is a majestic
exception,
leading us to invent
in a tropical fantasy
polished Portuguese merchants
captivated by Ashanti
golden jewels
and ivory filigree.
Telescopes scan the horizon
from fabulous towers.

But Elmina is also terrible
dungeons,
slave graveyards
and the shame of Europe.
The dwelling of bats
now,
like the objectification
of an animist ritual.

Vudu mon amour.

Cerca del puente levadizo,
un vendedor
callejero nos ofrece una estrella
de mar
a cambio de unas monedas.

Las enormes canoas de los pescadores
regresan
enarbolando ficticias banderas de color.
Vistoso capricho barroco
o sobredosis de símbolo:
Una acuarela de Malcolm Morley.

Los pescadores cantan
—y sus voces guturales nos transportan
al Caribe,
ahora a La Habana,
luego a Nueva Orleans—,
mientras descargan
peces espada
sobre la arena
acechados por el plumaje pardo
de los buitres.

La línea infinita de los cocoteros
frente al mar
es espejo del horizonte.

Near the drawbridge
a street-seller
offers us
a starfish
for a few coins.

The huge canoes of the fishermen
return
hoisting fictitious coloured flags.
A flashy baroque whim
or excess of symbol:
a watercolour by Malcolm Morley.

The fishermen are singing—
and their guttural voices transport us
to the Caribbean,
now to Havana,
then to New Orleans —,
while they unload
sword fish
on the sand
stalked by the shadowy plumage
of vultures.

The endless line of the coco-nut trees
fronting the sea
mirrors the horizon.

Automóvil con gato

para Flan Flanagan y Jessica Craig-Martin

Massive Attack a toda pastilla
desde una casa georgiana
en Hyde Park Corner...

La joven descalza
sobre la acera
con un vestido arrugado
de seda azul.

Cuelga de su mano
un único zapato de tacón
afilado y metálico,
larguísimo.

Se balancea
hacia un deportivo
verde,
cuando,
durante un solo instante,
un tímido rayo
de sol
ilumina sus ojos,
entornados,
enigmáticos.

El rostro de Londres
es de oro y miel.

Car with Cat

for Flan Flanagan and Jessica Craig-Martin

Massive Attack at full blast
from a Georgian house
at Hyde Park Corner.

The barefoot girl
on the pavement
in a ruckled dress
of blue silk.

From her hand
hangs a single high-heeled
shoe, sharp and metallic,
extremely long.

She is swaying
toward a green
sports car,
when,
for an instant,
a diffident sunray
lights up her eyes,
half-closed,
puzzling.

The face of London
is golden, honey-coloured.

La dávida

Poseído
por el ruido
de los zocos
nocturnos:
dátiles secos
y azúcar líquido
te liberan
del Ramadán.

Al amanecer:
dromedarios,
lentos turbantes,
falucas etéreas
bajo esta luz,
fuego invisible.

Frente al templo,
se oye la voz suprema
de la cantante del mundo.

Una avenida de esfinges,
árboles como espirales eléctricas,
escarabajos sagrados,
y los colores que velaron las momias.

La casa de Howard Carter,
como estatua de sal,
vuelta hacia las columnas
de piedra.

Colinas luminosas,
leyendas de alabastro,
Nilo larguísimo…

The Gift

Captivated
by the noise
of the night-time
zouk:
dried dates
and liquid sugar
free you
from Ramadan.

At dawn:
camels,
lethargic turbans,
ethereal *falucas*
under this light,
an invisible fire.

In front of the temple
the supreme voice
of the world's singer
can be heard.

An avenue of sphinxes,
trees like electric spirals,
sacred scarabs,
and colours that watched over mummies.

Howard Carter's house,
like a statue of salt,
facing columns
of stone.

Luminous hills,
alabaster legends,
the longest Nile ...

Luciérnagas para el ajolote

Las caracolas invocan una brújula
virtual
en un recinto sagrado maya
donde las brasas anticipan la luna
llena.

Júpiter es un hombre joven
que conduce el ritual del temaxcal.
El ocelote, el oso y el búfalo son invocados:
conceptos de muerte y transfiguración.

Los cuerpos ardientes
se sumergen después en las aguas
gélidas
y transparentes
del cenote.

Silencio magnífico del agua
cuando descienden luciérnagas,
chispas y colibríes de una compañía aérea
enana
sobre el mundo cavernario
de los peces ciegos.

La oscuridad es la luz.
Ardor espumoso
y tiempo helado:
un único espíritu.

Glow-Worms for the Axolot

The snails invoke a virtual
compass
in a sacred Mayan site
where embers anticipate
the full moon.

Jupiter is a young man
who leads the *Temaxcal* ritual.
The ocelot, the bear and the buffalo
are invoked:
concepts of death transfiguration.

Burning bodies
are submerged then in the icy
and lucent waters
of the *cenote*.

Magnificent silence of water
when glow-worms come down,
sparks and hummingbirds
of a dwarf
aerial squadron
over the cavernous world
of blind fish.

Darkness is light.
Frothy ardour
and frozen time:
a single spirit.

Mantra del amor y del éxtasis

Twirl
Palladium
J's Hangout
Xenon
Queen
Hôpital Éphémère
Distrito
James Dean
Metro
La Terraza
Zone DK
Heaven
The Fridge
Kingsway Hotel
Este Bar
The Break
Cha Cha
G
Splash
Roxy's
La Piscina
Picasso
Fellini
Morocco
Midway
Alien
Bus Stop
Venial
Twilo
Apolo
Stars
Tunnel
La Oficina

Mantra for Love and Esctasy

Twirl
Palladium
J's Hangout
Xenon
Queen
Hôpital Éphémère
Distrito
James Dean
Metro
La Terraza
Zone DK
Heaven
The Fridge
Kingsway Hotel
Este Bar
The Break
Cha Cha
G
Splash
Roxy's
La Piscina
Picasso
Fellini
Morocco
Midway
Alien
Bus Stop
Venial
Twilo
Apolo
Stars
Tunnel
La Oficina

Members
Ministry of Sound
Barracuda
Ricky's
Taller
Camp
Sound Factory
Black Cat
Biarritz
Moog
Blue Boy
Castropol
La Guerra
El Antro
Lost City
Coco Latte
Trade
Foxy
Coppelia
Ohm

(repetir en su totalidad hasta la victoria del sueño)

Members
Ministry of Sound
Barracuda
Ricky's
Taller
Camp
Sound Factory
Black Cat
Biarritz
Moog
Blue Boy
Castropol
La Guerra
El Antro
Lost City
Coco Latte
Trade
Foxy
Coppelia
Ohm

(to be repeated in its totality until sleep overcomes)

El meridiano de la desesperanza

para Sebastián Camps

Las huellas del saurio
sobre la arena
dibujan jeroglíficos extraños,
pistas alargadísimas
o dameros excéntricos
sobre los que crecen hongos
diminutos.
Peones vegetales
que juegan a ajedrez
con fragmentos multiformes de coral
muerto.

Rosa pálido bajo los árboles
preciosos
y repletos de pájaros
entre lianas
que forman arabescos,
drippings pollockianos...

(ahora me acuerdo tanto
de los poemas tropicales
de Sarduy)

La condensación del agua
forma cordilleras de nubes
sobre la selva.
El verde, el gris y el azul
como jamás los había visto...

Naturaleza:
murciélagos como frutas,
monos histéricos,

The Meridian of Despair

for Sebastián Camps

The traces of the saurian
on the sand
sketch strange hieroglyphs,
lengthy trails
or eccentric draught-boards
on which tiny fungi grow.
Vegetal pawns
playing chess
with multiform fragments
of dead coral.

Pale pink under trees
precious and
full of birds
amid lianas
forming arabesques
and Pollockian drippings ...

(I recall now so much
of the tropical poems
of Severo Sarduy)

The condensation of water
forms cordilleras of cloud
above the rain forest.
Green, grey and blue
as I have never seen before ...

Nature:
bats like fruit,
hysterical monkeys,

mariposas a cámara lenta,
y águilas pescadoras en la niebla
como solos de flauta
destacándose sobre una gran orquesta.

El silencio sonoro del viento
y una sobredosis de plantas…

Constelaciones gigantes
nos cubren como un pez manta
durante la luna nueva…

Negrísimas
son entonces las copas estrelladas
de los cocoteros que se mecen,
y las rocas
que viven sólo en la noche
cuando la marea baja,
alejando quizás a los tiburones,
y encallando las canoas
tristes.

Hace calor.

Oigo música china tan empalagosa
como el aire que me envuelve.

(ni Novalis, ni Friedrich,
ni Guillén, ni Rothko)

Recuerdo los colores vivientes
de un día dedicado a los jardines de coral.

Ahora buceo en la forma de las formas.

El lenguaje es el mundo.

dilatory butterflies,
and sea eagles in the mist
like flute solos
outstanding over a large orchestra.

The sonorous silence of the wind
and an excess of plants.

Gigantic constellations
cover us like a manta ray
during the new moon ...

The swaying coco-nut trees
are then pitch black
and the rocks
that come alive at night
when the tide is low,
maybe distancing the sharks
and stranding the canoes.

It's hot.

I hear Chinese music as cloying
as the air that envelops me.

(neither Novalis nor Friedrich,
neither Guillén nor Rothko)

I recall the vivid colours
of a day devoted to coral gardens.

Now I dive into the form of forms.

Language is the world.

La ciudad perdida

Fassbinder es el fantasma de Chinatown
cuando las putas de Kuala Lumpur
sienten terror hacia los hombres grandes
porque son angostas.

Las travestis se pelean
ante el cajero del Hong-Kong Bank
para atraer a clientes
electrónicos y plásticos.

Camisetas de Prada
y sofás de leopardo
en el interior de mercedes gigantes
a la puerta de un after.

Éxtasis tailandeses,
piel de melocotón
y ojos azabache.

Reyerta temible con la mafia china
cuando la noche es una sopa ardiente,
atronadora música tecno de *Lost City*.

Lost City

Fassbinder is the ghost of Chinatown
when the Kuala Lumpur whores
are terrified of big men
because they are narrow.

Drag-queens quarrel
at the Hong Kong Bank ATM
to attract electronic
and plastic clients.

Prada t-shirts
and leopard-skin seating
inside a giant Mercedes
at the door of the after-hours club.

Thai ecstasies,
peach skin
and jet-black eyes.

A ferocious brawl with the Chinese mafia
when night is a scalding soup,
deafening techno-music of *Lost City*.

Happy Together

para Orlando Hurtado

Un rectángulo azul flota
sobre un espacio naranja
rayado en oro.

Seda ritual y antigua,
que explica misterios antiguos.

Aquí hay hoy rascacielos de vidrio,
minaretes gulliver,
entrevistos desde el jardín.

Heliconias: la naturaleza imitando el plástico.

Imperio, también, magnífico ese parque,
de mariposas derrotadas,
donde las señoritas chinas
adoran joyas de titanio,
y conducen bmws
escuchando las músicas
de Wong Kar-Wai.

Faro, cascada y tango.

A toda velocidad
por la autopista
hacia los fuertes rojos que dejó Holanda.

La melancolía se funde con la niebla,
perfecta propietaria de infinita
plantación de caucho abandonada
a los ímpetus telúricos de la jungla.

Happy Together

for Orlando Hurtado

A blue rectangle floats
over an orange space
streaked with gold.

Ritual and antique silk
explaining ancient mysteries.

Here today are glass skyscrapers,
Gulliver minarets,
half-seen from the garden.

Heliconias:
nature mimicking plastic.

Also, an empire that park
of ruined butterflies,
where Chinese maidens
adore titanian jewels
and drive BMWs
to the music
of Wong Kar-Wai films.

Lighthouse, waterfall, tango.

At full speed
along the motorway
toward the red forts the Dutch left.

Melancholy fuses with the mist,
the perfect propriator
of a vast rubber plantation
deserted in the telluric powers of the jungle.

Los arrecifes nocturnos

para Pablo Pascual

Las flores hundidas en el barro
dibujan senderos en el bosque
para furtivos pies incendiarios.

Martín pescador y orquídea
aquí con inusitada frecuencia.

Los karaokes chinos
rugen toda la noche,
sin provocar el menor movimiento
de los árboles negros.

Los cuerpos se buscan.

De pronto,
evocación del escualo y hamaca tensa:
tálamo telaraña.

Orgías de caucho,
con tridente y buzo,
sobre la helada arena triunfante
y la selva toronja.

Nocturnal Reefs

for Pablo Pascual

Flowers sunk in the mud
draw paths in the forest
for furtive arsonist feet.

Kingfisher and orchids
are unusually frequent here.

Chinese karaokes
blaring all night,
the black trees
indifferently motionless.

Bodies seek each other.

Suddenly,
evocation of shark and tense hammock,
a spiderweb bridal bed.

Rubber orgies,
with trident and diver,
on the victorious frozen sand
and the grapefruit forest.

La guerra del opio en Marang

Los varanos se lanzan al agua
alejándose de las barcazas

Una aguila pescadora
flota en el aire
y su sombra oculta
por un instante
el polvo blanco
en las manos
de los piratas.

Monos que aúllan,
envolviendo a turistas inocentes
y cebúes que aman a Brancusi
locamente.

El olor espantoso de las frutas
con pieles reptiles,
alacranes de cuarzo
y espumas atávicas.

Tus ojos como celosías persas:
disparos en el paraíso
entre las más altas cometas blancas.

The Opium War in Marang

The monitor lizards dive
moving off from the barges.

A sea eagle
floats in the air
and its shadow
momentarily
hides
the white powder
on the pirates'
hands.

Howler monkeys
surround innocent tourists
and zebus madly in love
with Brancusi.

The frightful smell of the fruit
with reptilian skin,
quartz scorpions
and atavistic foam.

Your eyes Persian lattice,
gunshots in paradise
amid the highest white comets.

Dakar

La ciudad crepuscular
repleta de gente
mientras las rapaces cubren el cielo
con plumas negras.

Turbantes y túnicas brillantes
semiocultos entre sombras.

Un pez espada de neón
al pie del acantilado.

Villas neoplasticistas,
cocoteros
y buganvillas tricolores:
rojo, fucsia y violeta.

La noche repleta del erotismo
de los tambores,
que hacen de los cuerpos
sus esclavos contorsionistas.

Un baobab solitario
absorbe la oscuridad del cielo.

Música hipnótica y alcohol,
luz incierta,
las olas embravecidas del océano
y una luna magnífica.

No espero a nadie,
pero insisto que alguien tiene que llegar.

Dakar

The twilight city
crowded with people
while birds of prey cover the sky
with their black feathers.

Turbans and bright tunics
half-hidden in shadows.

A neon sword fish
at the foot of the cliff.

Neo-plasticist villas,
coco-nut trees
and tri-colour bougainvilleas:
red, fuchsia and purple.

Night is full of the eroticism
of the drums
that make bodies
their contortionist slaves.

A solitary baobab
absorbs the darkness of the sky.

Hypnotic music and alcohol,
uncertain light,
the furious waves of the ocean
and a magnificent moon.

I am waiting for no one
but I insist someone must arrive.

La música del sentido

*Toda verdadera música procede del llanto, pusto
que ha nacido de la nostalgia del paraíso.*
—E.M. Cioran

Music of Sense

All true music comes from lament
since it was born from the longing for paradise.
—E.M.Cioran

Autorretrato con 39 años

Conozco centenares de clubs de jazz desiertos,
hoteles coloniales
palacios ajados
y todas las embajadas del mundo.

He buscado en ruinas milenarias,
en bibliotecas,
en arrecifes de coral,
en junglas y desiertos.

He bebido y me he drogado
hasta perder la consciencia
y he follado con centenares de cuerpos.

Hoy sé, sin embargo, que ya lo tenía todo
dentro.

Self-Portrait at 39

I know hundreds of deserted jazz clubs,
colonial hotels, old palaces
and all the embassies of the world.

I have searched in millenary ruins,
in libraries,
in coral reefs,
in jungles and deserts.

I have drunk and taken drugs
to unconsciousness
and I had sex with hundreds of bodies.

I know now, however,
I had everything
within me.

La luz negra

Tel Aviv…

La luz me persigue,
me aplasta sobre el asfalto.

No miro nada,
no escucho nada.
Camino entre villas bauhaus
y árboles tropicales.

Una energía nueva me recorre el cuerpo
y me nubla la cabeza.

Las lágrimas me arrancan el alma.
La energía se me escapa por los dedos,
Y mi espíritu, por fin, mira mi cuerpo
desde la azotea del hotel.

Lloro en una brutal sucesión de espasmos.
No ando en ninguna dirección
ni busco nada.
Tampoco sé dónde estoy
pero no me importa.
Las nubes me vuelven loco
ofreciéndomelo todo.

Le recuerdo:
Cuando baila solo entre la gente
su cuerpo se me antoja de plata.
Le grito que no me deje y se me escapa.
Todo es infinito e invisible.

Black Light

Tel Aviv …

Light pursues me
crushing me against the asphalt.

I am looking at nothing,
I am listening to nothing,

I walk among Bauhaus villas
and tropical trees.

A new energy races through my body
clouding my brain.

Tears draw out my soul.
Energy escapes through my fingers,
and my spirit, finally, looks at my body
from the roof of the hotel.

I cry in a brutal succession of spasms.
I am walking nowhere in particular
nor looking for anything.
Neither do I know where I am
but I couldn't care less.
The clouds drive me crazy
offering me everything.

I remember him:
when he dances alone among the crowd
I imagine his body is silver.
I shout at him not to leave me
but he escapes.
Everything is infinite and invisible.

Amo sus ojos,
manchados, caídos, tristes
poseídos por la luna.

Y ahora la luz me atrapa:
Me veo por dentro
y mi cuerpo es un animal muerto
de hambre.
No puedo enseñárselo
porque me da la espalda.

Entonces toda la luz se escapa
por las rendijas del laberinto insondable del espíritu.

Estoy sólo.
Un dolor tremendo
me vuelve el alma negra.

I love his eyes,
speckled, fallen, sad,
entranced by the moon.

And now the light snares me.
I see inside myself
and my body is a dead, starved animal.

I cannot show it to him
for he turns his back on me.

Then all light escapes
through the clefts
of the unfathomable labyrinth
of the spirit.

I am alone.

A tremendous grief
turns my soul black.

Amor

Lloro a cada rato
y me miro en un espejo
sin reconocer mi rostro.

Deseo tus labios
y tu espíritu,
los miembros me tiemblan
y me abro por dentro.

Tengo visiones:
caras que se alejan,
luces rojas y amarillas,
espirales inmensas
y glaciares muertos.

Soy el aire y la lluvia
y sólo hacia adentro puedo
llegar a ti.

Love

I can't stop crying
and I look in a mirror
without recognizing myself.

I desire your lips
and your spirit,
my members trembles
and I open up.

I have visions:
faces moving off,
red and yellow lights,
immense spirals
and dead glaciers.

I am air and rain
and can only reach you
inwardly.

La casa del los amigos

(Frederik Kiesler y James Turrell en el Museo Israel de Jersusalén)

para Juan Manuel Bonet

Arde el sol
y busco cavernas.
Espacios recogidos y misteriosos
que me ayuden a explorar mi alma.

El laberinto de Kiesler
me sobrecoge,
se aprovecha de mi nueva consciencia.
Desemboca en una cúpula blanca
cuya luz lunar es alabastro.
Un espacio circular
con desniveles
que me anima a adentrarme
en mí mismo.

De nuevo las lágrimas
espasmódicas
de esta felicidad extraña.

A continuación me encuentro a Turrell:
un espacio que mira
un cielo hoy tan nuboso.

Me tumbo boca arriba
un largo tiempo
y siento como mi sangre
bombea las masas blancas
de las nubes
que se desplazan
y me envuelven

The House of Friends

(Frederik Kiesler and James Turrell at the Israeli Museum in Jerusalem)

for Juan Manual Bonet

The sun is burning
and I am searching for caverns.
Secluded and mysterious spaces
to help me explore my soul.

Kiesler's labyrinth
overwhelms me,
exploits my new consciousness.
It leads into a white dome
whose lunar light is alabaster.
A circular uneven space
that excites me
to go into myself.

Again tears
spasmodic
with this strange happiness.

Ahead, I meet Turrell:
a space that looks at
the sky so cloudy today.

I lie down on my back
for a long time
and I feel my blood
pumping the white masses
of clouds stirring
and they envelop me

con una alegría diáfana.
Soy muy grande.
También enormemente pequeño.

in a diaphanous joy.
I am huge,
but also enormously small.

Muecín y abeja

Disfruto perdiéndome
por los callejones oscuros
 y estrechos
del zoco de Jerusalén.
Adivino especias
y me dejo llevar
por músicas exóticas.

Por fin una pequeña plaza
con árboles que se mecen
al vaivén de la brisa.

Compro un zumo de naranja
y su aroma atrae a una abeja.
Entonces la voz del muecín
dibuja metales sobre el cielo
que me parten como espadas.

Soy un insecto
y no hago nada.
Quiero dejarme llevar por un viento poderoso.

Muezzin and Bee

I enjoy losing myself
in the dark and narrow alleyways
of the Jerusalem zouk.
I guess at spices
and I let myself be borne away
on exotic rhythms.

At last a small square
with trees swaying
to the whim of slight wind.

I buy an orange juice
and its aroma attracts a bee.
Then the voice of the muezzin
draws metals on the sky
that divide me like a sword.

I am an insect
and I do nothing.
I want to be carried away by a powerful wind.

A un hombre solo conduciendo un deportivo azul

"Encantador de cobras,
si me miras una parte de mí adquiere vida propia".

"Traficante de esclavos,
si me tocas puedes venderme en los confines del mundo".

"Asesino implacable,
si me besas conozco el sentido último del hielo".

Impávido,
despreciando tu belleza,
me contestas:
"No existe ni el espacio ni el tiempo".

Me desconciertas
un instante,
pero aún sé
que contigo
todo es mar
embravecido.

Te lo ruego,
perdona este deseo
impuro,
déjame ser tu tabla de surf.

To a Lonely Man Driving a Blue Sportscar

'Cobra charmer,
if you look at me, a part of me acquires its own life.'

'Slave trader,
if you touch me, you can sell me the world over.'

'Implacable killer,
if you kiss me, I know the ultimate meaning of ice.'

Fearless,
despising your own beauty,
you answer:
'Neither time nor space exist.'

You upset me
for a moment
but still I know
that with you
everything
is a crashing sea.

I beseech you,
forgive this
impure;
let me be your surf board.

Torso de neón

Lloras tumbado en el sofá
acurrucado entre mis brazos,
tocando el fondo de las cosas
o su apariencia vacía,
devastadora.

Me dices que no me amas
ni me amarás nunca,
que nos ata un invisible lazo
espiritual,
eterno.

Te encuentras solo,
y reclamas el calor
que puedo darte.

Abrazo tu torso musculado,
adivino el sol de la carne,
y el fuego me aniquila
por dentro.
Me hundo en inmensos océanos,
ardientes, espesos, negros.

Una luz invisible
se me escapa
por todos los orificios del cuerpo,
brasa convertida en neón
al rodear a un hombre de hielo.
Al fin forma un receptáculo
reparador,
capaz de detener el tiempo.

Oigo tu respiración
y me concentro en ella.

Neon Torso

You cry stretched on the sofa
huddling in my arms,
touching the depth of things
or its appearance
empty and devastating.

You tell me you don't love
and that you'll never love,
but that we are bound by an invisible
spiritual bond.

You are alone
and you claim the warmth
I can give you.

I embrace your muscular torso,
I foresee the sun of the flesh,
and fire annihilates me
internally.
I sink in immense oceans,
burning, turgid, black.

An invisible light
escapes
through all the orifices my body,
ember becomes neon
on embracing a man of ice.
Then it becomes a mending
receptacle,
able to stop time.

I hear your breathing
and I concentrate on it.

Me pierdo en una noche de luz,
ajeno a la conjunción
maravillosa
del ártico y del trópico.

Esto sucede
en un mismo punto eterno.

Uno tiene que morir
para salvar al otro.

La vida
ni es todo ni es nada.

I lose myself in a night of light
estranged from the marvelous
conjunction
of the arctic and the tropic.

This occurs
at the same eternal point.

One has to die
to save the other.

Life is neither everything nor nothing.

Deseo

Tus labios saben a cilantro
y a búfalo.

Mis huesos se deshacen
en armónicos
inconexos
y caen metales
masivos
del aire.

Tus ojos son un infinito
crepúsculo púrpura
robado del estaño
de los lagos altos.

Lo veo todo
desde un avión,
y las estepas del tiempo
no son sino nubes
blandas
que me envuelven
y que traspaso
sin dificultad aparente.

Toco el horizonte,
maravillado,
con las palmas de las manos.

El orgasmo sólo puede ser una oración.

Desire

Your lips taste like coriander
and buffalo.

My bones are undone
in unconnected
harmonies
and massive metals
fall
from the air.

Your eyes are an infinite
purple twilight
stolen from the tin
of the high lakes.

I see everything
from an airplane,
and the steppes of time
are no more than
white clouds
that envelop me
and I pass through
with apparent ease.

I touch the horizon,
amazed,
with the palms of my hands.

Orgasm can only be a prayer.

Los gusanos

Hace días que no te veo
y que tampoco hablamos.

Me rodeo de libros.
Sin embargo, la literatura no es
evasión.

Gabriel Ferrater:
cuando los gusanos cenen
mi cuerpo
todavía
encontraran algo
de tu sabor.

The Worms

It is some days since I saw you
and neither did we speak.

I surround myself with books.
Yet literature is not
an escape.

Gabriel Ferrater:
when the worm dine
on my body,
they will still find
something
of your flavour.

Biblioteca para una isla desierta

Walter Abish
César Aira
James Baldwin
Roland Barthes
Djuna Barnes
William Boyd
E.M. Cioran
Julio Cortázar
San Juan de la Cruz
Mircea Eliade
Luis de Góngora
Amitav Ghosh
Juan Goytisolo
Jorge Guillén
Romesh Gunesekera
Alfred Jarry
James Joyce
C.S. Jung
Ernst Jünger
Valéry Larbaud
José Lezama Lima
Clarice Lispector
Stéphane Mallarmé
Herman Melville
Ian McEwan
Jay McInerney
Álvaro Mutis
Vladimir Nabokov
Carlos Pellicer
Anthony Powell
Marcel Proust
Alain Robbe-Grillet
Severo Sarduy

Library for a Desert Island

Walter Abish
César Aira
James Baldwin
Roland Barthes
Djuna Barnes
William Boyd
E.M. Cioran
Julio Cortázar
San Juan de la Cruz
Mircea Eliade
Luis de Góngora
Amitav Ghosh
Juan Goytisolo
Jorge Guillén
Romesh Gunesekera
Alfred Jarry
James Joyce
C.G. Jung
Ernst Jünger
Valéry Larbaud
José Lezama Lima
Clarice Lispector
Stéphane Mallarmé
Herman Melville
Ian McEwan
Jay McInerney
Alvaro Mutis
Vladimir Nabokov
Carlos Pellicer
Anthony Powell
Marcel Proust
Alain Robbe-Grillet
Severo Sarduy

Francis Scott-Fitzgerald
Stendhal
Wallace Stevens
Alfonsina Storni
Junichiro Tanizaki
Giusseppe Ungaretti
Enrique Vila-Matas
Evelyn Waugh

Francis Scott-Fitzgerald
Stendhal
Wallace Stevens
Alfonsina Storni
Junichiro Tanizaki
Giusseppe Ungaretti
Enrique Vila-Matas
Evelyn Waugh

La noche insular

para Terry Winters y Hendel Teicher

Trocadero 162:
los libros del coronel
y el diminuto vaso danés,
el gamo de madera
y el cofre de plata peruano,
los retratos de Martí, Góngora, Mallarmé.

Un cocotero azul
con ojos de gato
en un jardín invisible
proclama que la muerte no existe
(adios a Heidegger).

El poeta inmóvil
está, entonces, dentro de mí.
Nada abrazado a un cocodrilo
gigante
y de su boca salen
todas las palabras del mundo.

Columna
sin fin
ascendente
este chorro de luz.

Renacer aquí
es un placer innombrable.

Insular Night

for Terry Winters and Hendel Teicher

Trocadero 162:
the colonel's books
and the small Danish vase,
the wooden deer
and the Peruvian silver chest,
the portraits of Martí, Góngora, Mallarmé.

A blue coconut-tree
with feline eyes
in an invisible garden
declares that death does not exist
(bye-bye Heidegger).

The poet is, then,
motionless inside me.
He swims in the embrace
of a giant crocodile
and all the words of the world
emerge from his mouth.

Endless
column
ascending
this stream of light.

To be reborn here
is an unnameable pleasure.

Terra Lucida

Respiro
sin pensar
entre pegajosas constelaciones negras.
Astros y nubes
en un océano de aire.

Mi cuerpo flota
convertido en luz.

Soy un film:
Cabezas de modelos enterradas
picoteadas por rápidas gallinas
verdes.

Luego, una playa
en la India
que será mi casa siempre.

Me acompaña un perro
blanco
y ambos volamos sin alas.
Rostros desconocidos me protegen.

Todo es extraño y familiar.

Me veo emanando fuego.

Camino bajo cascadas de hielo
hacia las espirales naranja.

Soy el cielo,
pues me abrazo y me convierto en él.

Terra Lucida

I breathe
thoughtlessly
amid black clinging constellations.
Stars and clouds
in an ocean of air.

My float floats
changed into light.

I am a film:
heads of buried models
pecked by swift green
hens.

Then, a beach in India
that will always be my home.

A white dog
keeps my company
and we both fly without wings.
Unknown faces protect me.

Everything is strange and familiar.

I see myself emanating fire.

I walk under waterfalls of ice
toward the orange spirals.

I am the sky
since I embrace myself and become it.

BAHÍA DE LAS BANDERAS (2007)

BAY OF FLAGS (2007)

Noches con mares griegos en que el ruido
del hidroavión de plata de Odiseo
suscita huelgas en los altos nidos.
—Carlos Pellicer

Dispérsame en la lluvia o en la humareda de los torrentes que
pasan
—César Moro

Y en silencio salen ángeles de los azules
ojos de los amantes que sufren más dulcemente
—Georg Trakl

no lejos de la noche
mi cuerpo mudo
se abre
a la delicada urgencia del rocío
—Alejandra Pizarnik

Nights with Greek seas in which the noise
of the silver seaplane of Odysseus
agitates strikes in the high nests.
—Carlos Pellicer

Scatter me in the rain or in the smoke-cloud of coursing streams
—César Moro

And angels in silence emerge from the blue
eyes of lovers who suffer more sweetly
—Georg Trakl

Not far from night
my deaf body
opens up
to the delicate urgency of dew
—Alejandra Pizarnik

Fuegos

1

Hoy,
tras dos días
soleados
y fríos,
por fin,
llueve.

Miro los edificios grises
y te hablo
cruzando el río Liffey.
Las calles están llenas
de la gente de los sábados.

Acaba de salir el disco nuevo
de Massive Attack:
himnos hipnóticos
con mariposas atrapadas.
Ambar,
ésta narcosis dulce.
Sílabas deslumbrantes
y huracanes amarillos.

Lo escucho en el hotel
leyendo el *País de Nieve*
de Yasunari Kawabata.

Faltan siete días
para tenerte conmigo
y tiemblo cuando pienso
que llegas por la noche
a nuestra casa nueva.

Fires

1

Today,
after two
sunny
and cold days,
finally,
it rains.

I look at the grey buildings
and I talk to you
as I cross the River Liffey.
The streets are full
of Saturday crowds.

A new CD of *Massive Attack*
has just been released:
hypnotic hymns
with trapped butterflies.
Amber,
this sweet narcosis.
Dazzling syllables
and yellow hurricanes.

I'm listening to it in the hotel
as I read Yasunari Kawabata's
Snow Country.

Seven days to go
before I meet you
and I tremble when I think
you'll arrive at night
at our new house.

El cuerpo me pesa
durante un tiempo.
Luego,
poco a poco,
el fondo de las cosas
se vuelve agua.

Un viento helado
sacude rocas gigantes
y los pájaros son
naipes quebradizos.

2

No te lo dije aún
porque no sabes quién es,
pero le conocí nada más llegar
a Dublín.

Fui a una galería
a conocer las versiones
de Arcadia
—ánades, bosques
y bañistas modélicas—,
de un amigo de Juan Navarro Baldeweg.

Adecuadamente estaba allí
el poeta del norte y de la luz eléctrica:
Sólo pude cruzar
unas pocas palabras con él,
rodeado como estaba de gente,
pero verle me pareció un buen augurio.
Recordé entonces un sueño
que tuvo una amiga de Madrid:

For a while
my body feels leaden.
Then,
little by little,
in the depth of things,
it becomes water.

A freezing wind
stirs gigantic boulders
and birds are
a pack of frail cards.

2

I haven't told you yet
because you don't know who he is,
but I met him
on my first night
in Dublin.

I went to a gallery
to get to know
the versions of Arcadia
—mallards, woods
and model bathers—
by a friend of Juan Navarro Baldeweg.

It was enough he was there,
the poet of the North and Electric Light:
I could only pass
a few words with him,
surrounded as he was by people,
but to see him seemed a good sign to me.
I recalled then a dream
a friend of mine from Madrid had:

Un sendero de luces
mojadas,
en un mundo en que las liebres
derrotan a los trenes,
conducía a una habitación
en la que yo era oráculo.

Mientras tanto:
pantanos profundos,
líquenes y musgos
como susurros delirantes.

Cabezas de ciervos
y cerveza de obsidiana.

3

Es domingo
y el sol es un disco de oro
horadando un bloque de hielo.

Me siento un ermitaño
lejos de las voces de los amigos.

Una y otra vez,
sin embargo,
te veo nadando
en una playa solitaria,
avanzando veloz
hacia el horizonte,
o encendiendo la arena
con diminutas llamas azules.

A path of damp
lights,
in a world where hares
outrace trains,
led to a room
in which I was an oracle.

In the meantime:
deep swamps,
lichens and mosses
like delirious sighs.

Heads of deer
and obsidian beer.

3

It's Sunday
and the sun is a golden disk
drilling a block of ice.

I feel myself a hermit
remote from the voices of my friends.

From time to time,
however,
I see you swimming
off a solitary beach,
moving swiftly
toward the horizon,
or burning the sand
with small blue flames.

Cuando se va la luz,
el mundo es un muro
de música sintética.
Un ritmo de agujas,
cristal
y agua
marcado por un contrabajo
púrpura.

He visto una película de Martin Scorsese
realmente horrible.
Sin embargo, la llovizna helada
sobre mi cara
es la misma que te salpica a ti.

4

Al despertar
cuervos y gaviotas
juegan al ajedrez
sobre la hierba.

Habitaciones, sábanas,
lenguas y dientes.

El museo donde vivo
es idéntico
a los jardines de Marienbad.

Un crimen
sin culpables
y que secuencia el tiempo
en imágenes perdurables
sin principio ni fin.

When the light goes,
the world is a wall
of synthetic music.
A rhythm of needles,
glass
and water
stamped with a purple
double bass.

I have seen a really horrible
Marin Scorsese film.
But the freezing drizzle
on my face
is the same that splashes you.

4

As I wake,
crows and seagulls
play chess
on the grass.

Rooms, sheets,
tongues and teeth.

The museum where I live
is identical
with the gardens of Marienbad.

A crime
without the guilty
and a temporal sequence
in lasting images
without beginning or end.

5

Zurich es el Museo Rietberg
y nuestra casa la Villa Wessendonck.
Hay nieve neoclásica sobre el césped
cerca del lago que refleja montañas.

La silla de Wagner
en la habitación de Shiva
contempla yates
convertidos en patos.

En el sótano,
Utamaro:
miembros enormes
sobre los que se sientan las geishas.
Un mundo de seda lenta
y sonidos alámbricos.

Luego, pinturas indias.
Árboles y plantas
como signos
en habitaciones transparentes
y geométricas.
Hay tórtolas,
monos,
elefantes.

El agua de las fuentes
dirige la música de los cuerpos.
Sólo para los griegos
el sexo es una competición.

Tu cuerpo
destruye
todo paradigma histórico.

5

Zurich is the Rietberg Museum
and our house the Villa Wessendonck.
There is neoclassical snow on the lawn
near the lake reflecting the mountains.

The chair of Wagner
in the room of Shiva
contemplates yachts
changed into ducks.

In the cellar,
Utamaro:
huge penises
on which geishas sit.
A world of slow silk
and wiry sounds.

Later, Indian paintings.
Trees and plants
like signs
in transparent
and geometric rooms.
There are turtledoves,
monkeys,
elephants.

The fountain's water
conducts the music of bodies.

Sex is a competition
only for the Greeks.

Your body
destroys
every historic paradigm.

Después de ver 2046

Una idea de la felicidad:
Oppiano Licario
dirigida por Wong Kar-Wai.

After Seeing 2046

An idea of happiness:
Oppiano Licario
directed by Wong Kar-Wai.

Los ojos del ángel

Por la mañana, al despertarse,
el agua que besa la arena blanca.

Durante el amor, la historia entera
de la arquitectura de la India.

Enfadado, los ritmos turbios
del *hip-hop,* y cuando triste
un magnánimo arco iris.

Si me pierdo que me busquen allí.

The Angel Eyes

In the morning, as I wake up,
like water kissing the white sand.

During lovemaking, the whole history
of India's architecture.

Angry: the turbulent rhythms
of *hip-hop*. Sad:
a magnanimous rainbow.

If I get lost, let them find me there.

África

para Victor Esposito

El tiempo es un ornamento
tallado en el aire
por las manos de los percusionistas.

Africa es el centro del mundo.

Ojos que incendian la sabana,
fuego verde,
y los pantanos del delta
del Okavango.

Mi sangre es el agua
que rompe las piedras
de las que crecen plantas:
flores magníficas
en las yemas de los dedos.

Tu piel forma un universo
entero.
Seda hecha de estrellas
y trinos de pájaros.

Al final de todo sólo hay luz.

Africa

for Victor Esposito

Time is an ornament
carved in the air
by the hands of drummers.

Africa is the centre of the world.

Eyes that burn savannahs,
green fire,
and the delta swamps
of the Okavango.

My blood is water
that breaks stones
from which plants grow:
magnificent flowers
on fingers-tips.

Your skin forms an entire
universe.
Silk made of stars
and the trilling of birds.

At the end of all there is only light.

En el pabellón chino

He bebido
y te imagino
entrando en el bar:
se origina
el barroco portugués.

Pienso tu piel
y estoy entonces
en una orgía
con cien piratas negros.

Quiero hacer el amor contigo
toda la noche
y ver como después
te duermes confiado
entre mis brazos
sabiendo que cuando quiera
te puedo volver a tener.

In the Chinese Pavillion

I have drunk
and I imagine
you entering the bar:
it is the origin of
Portuguese Baroque.

I think about your skin
and then I am
in an orgy
with a hundred black pirates.

I want to make love with you
all night
and to see how later
you sleep securely
in my arms
knowing that when I wish
I can have you again.

El ángel asesino

para Bhupen Khakhar, in memoriam

Estoy muerto
y aún así me acuerdo de mi asesino:
luminoso
y con disfraz de ángel del cielo.

Cada recuerdo ahora,
empero, no es sino un obstáculo
escondido entre las sombras
de una tumba negra
e infinita.
Sí, cada recuerdo es un obstáculo
afilado y frío,
de hielo,
que me golpea brazos y piernas,
pero se derrite
doblemente cruel
por inasible.

Otras veces los recuerdos son
fogonazos de luz
violenta
que me ciegan
en esta jaula
oscura
y tornan toda visión
una pesadilla expresionista y sangrienta.

Tu sonrisa sobre el Gran Canal de Venecia y
cruzando el Bósforo en Estambul,
tus ojos dulces por la mañana
en la ducha o en la cama,

The Murderous Angel

for Bhupen Khakhar, in memoriam

I am dead
and even so I recall my murderer:
luminous
and in a heavenly angel's disguise.

Yet every morning now
is nothing but an obstacle
hidden among the shadows
of a black
and infinite tomb.
Every memory is
a sharp and cold obstacle,
icy,
that strikes my arms and legs,
but melts
doubly cruel
being ungraspable.

At other times memories
are flashes of violent
light
that blind me
in this dark cage
and turn all vision
into a gory expressionist nightmare.

Your smile over Venice's Grand Canal and
crossing the Bosphorus in Istambul,
your gentle eyes in the morning
in the shower or in bed,
your warm silhouette

tu silueta cálida cenando en un hotel vacío
en las cataratas Victoria,
y un día entero, solo contigo, en una playa vacía
de Ibiza
acariciándote dentro del agua.

Y por supuesto todas esas noches
que te tenía entre mis brazos
y escuchaba tu respiración
o tus palabras:
hablando de nuestra casa,
nuestro jardín y nuestro perro.

Fue una trampa terrible
prometer el amor
después de la muerte.

El amor es una casa que sólo existe en los sueños
y que yo imagino en la India
quizás porque nunca vaya a llegar allí:
playas vacías e inmensas
donde la nieve no es sino luciérnagas.

Quiero ser arena,
orquídeas muertas
y plumas de pájaros:
que al menos mis cenizas sean
blancas
disueltas en la espuma
de todas las horas negras.

as we dine in an empty hotel
in Victoria Falls,
and a whole day, alone with you, off a beach
in Ibiza
caressing you in the water.

And of course all those nights
when I held you in my arms
and listened to your breathing
or your words:
speaking of our house,
our garden and our dog.

It's a terrible trap
to promise love
after death.

Love is a house that only exists in dreams
and which I imagine in India
maybe because I'll never be there:
empty and vast beaches
where snow is nothing but glow-worms.

I want to be sand,
dead orchids
and bird feathers:
at least let my ashes
be white
dissolved in the foam
of all the black hours.

Eclipse

La luna llena
desaparece
durante una noche helada
en Minnesota
borrando su reflejo
sobre el agua

Solo,
contemplo ese vacío
negro
y el tiempo
no tiene límites.

Sé que estás allí
como la luna.

Eclipse

The full moon
disappears
during a freezing night
in Minnesota
erasing its reflection
on the water.

Alone,
I ponder that black
emptiness
and time
has no limits.

I know you are there
like the moon.

Autobiografía

Jalsaghar, Satyajit Ray
In the Mood for Love, Wong Kar-Wai
La Notte, Michelangelo Antonioni
L'Année dernier à Marienbad, Alain Resnais
El silencio, Ingmar Bergman
Ugetsu Monogatari, Kenji Mizoguchi
Intimate Lighting, Ivan Passer
Eyes Wide Shut, Stanley Kubrick
La niña santa, Lucrecia Martel
Yeleen, Souleiman Cissé
High and Low, Akira Kurosawa
Ordet, Carl T. Dreyer
Yellow Earth, Chen Kaige
La Dolce Vita, Federico Fellini
Hable con ella, Pedro Almodóvar
Blow-up, Michelangelo Antonioni
Solaris, Andrei Tarkovsky
Une chambre en ville, Jaques Demy
Dogville, Lars von Trier
The Trouble with Harry, Alfred Hitchcock
L'Avventura, Michelangelo Antonioni
Happy Together, Wong Kar-Wai
To Have and to Have Not, Howard Hawks
The Dead, John Huston
Keep Cool, Zhang Yimou
Cyclo, Tran Ann Hungh
Stalker, Andrei Tarkovski
La reina de la noche, Arturo Ripstein
Uzak, Nuri Bilge Ceylan
À bout de souffle, Jean-Luc Godard
Le Samouraï, Jean-Pierre Melville
Exotica, Atom Egoyan
La maman et la putain, Jean Eustache

Autobiography

Jalsaghar, Satyajit Ray
In the Mood for Love, Wong KarWai
La Notte, Michelangelo Antonioni
Last Year at Marienbad, Alain Resnais
The Silence, Ingmar Bergman
Ugetsu Monogatari, Kenji Mizoguchi
Intimate Lighting, Ivan Passer
Eyes Wide Shut, Stanley Kubrick
La niña santa, Luerecia Martel
Yeleen, Souleiman Cissé
High and Low, Akira Kurosawa
Ordet, Carl T. Dreyer
Yellow Earth, Chen Kaige
La Dolce Vita, Federico Fellini
Hable con ella, Pedro Almodóvar
Blow-up, Michelangelo Antonioni
Solaris, Andrei Tarkovsky
Une chambre en ville, Jaques Demy
Dogville, Lars von Trier
The Trouble with Harry, Alfred Hitcheock
L'Avventura, Michelangelo Antonioni
Happy Together, Wong KarWai
To Have and to Have Not, Howard Hawks
The Dead, John Huston
Keep Cool, Zhang Yimou
Cyclo, Tran Ann Hungh
Stalker, Andrei Tarkovski
La reina de la noche, Arturo Ripstein
Uzak, Nuri Bilge Ceylan
À bout de souffle, Jean-Luc Godard
Le Samouraï, Jean-Pierre Melville
Exotica, Atom Egoyan
La maman et la putain, Jean Eustache

Modesty Blaise, Joseph Losey
Partner, Bernardo Bertolucci
Days and Nights in the Forest, Satyajit Ray
Shakespeare Wallah, James Ivory
Touch of Evil, Orson Welles
Chinatown, Roman Polanski
Days of being Wild, Wong Kar-Wai
Las amargas lágrimas de Petra von Kant, Rainer Werner Fassbinder
L'Homme blessé, Patrice Chéreau
Last Life in the Universe, Pan Renteneurang
Bad Guy, Kim Ku-juk
Farenheit 451, François Truffaut
El manantial de la doncella, Ingmar Bergman
Aguirre, der Zorn Gottes, Werner Herzog xxx opposite in English?
The French Lieutenant's Woman, Karel Reisz
The Night of the Hunter, Charles Laughton
Teorema, Pier Paolo Pasolini
The Party, Blake Edwards
Werkmeister Harmonies, Béla Tarr
La mujer de las dunas, Hiroshi Teshigara
Tokio Story, Yasujiro Ozu
Cenizas y diamantes, Andrej Wajda
Rocco i el sui fratelli, Luchino Visconti xxx opposite in English
El ámigo americano, Wim Wenders
Mouchette, Robert Bresson
Stromboli, Roberto Rosselini
Dillinger è morto, Marco Ferreri
L'homme qui ment, Alain Robbe-Grillet xxx caps?
Un Chant d'Amour, Jean Genet
El joven Törless, Volker Schlondorf
The Servant, Joseph Losey
Babette's Feast, Gabriel Axel
Three Times, Hou Hsiao-Hsien
Apocalypse Now, Francis Ford Coppola

Modesty Blaise, Joseph Losey
Partner, Bernardo Bertolucci
Days and Nights in the Forest, Satyajit Ray
Shakespeare Wallah, James Ivory
Touch of Evil, Orson Welles
Chinatown, Roman Polanski
Days of being Wild, Wong KarWai
The bitter Tears of Petra von Kant, Rainer Werner Fassbinder
L'Homme blessé, Patrice Chéreau
Last Life in the Universe, Pan Renteneurang
Bad Guy, Kim Kujuk
Farenheit 451, Francois Truffaut
The Maiden Spring, Ingmar Bergman
Aguirre, the Wrath of God, Werner Herzog
The French Lieutenant's Woman, Karel Reisz
The Night of the Hunter, Charles Laughton
Teorema, Pier Paolo Pasolini
The Party, Blake Edwards
Werkmeister Harmonies, Béla Tarr
The Woman of the Dunes, Hiroshi Teshigara
Tokio Story, Yasujiro Ozu
Ashes and Diamonds, Andrej Wajda
Rocco and his Brothers, Luchino Visconti
The American Friend, Wim Wenders
Mouchette, Robert Bresson
Stromboli, Roberto Rosselini
Dillinger è morto, Mareo Ferreri
L'homme qui ment, Alain Robbe-Grillet
Un Chant d'Amour, Jean Genet
The Young Törless, Volker Schlondorf
The Servant, Joseph Losey
Babette's Feast, Gabriel Axel
Three Times, Hou Hsiao-Hsien
Apocalypse Now, Francis Ford Coppola

Bakhtapur

para Francesco Clemente

Sobre el tambor,
un dragón
tántrico
y tigres desventrados.

Una niña sagrada,
diosa ocasional,
se esconde
en el interior del templo.

La máscara es un panal
de avispas narcóticas
y el chamán se atiborra de miel
para volar sobre los acantilados.

Nos rodean varias
estupas de piedra
y los metales
vibran
indefinidamente.

Un tetera china
de esmalte negro
y monos
sobre collares de flores.

Un santón albino
se alimenta de leche
cerca de las piras
de los muertos.
Sobre la colina

Bakhtapur

for Francesco Clemente

On the drum,
a dragon
tantric,
and wretched tigers.

A sacred girl,
a casual goddess,
is concealed
in the interior of the temple.

The mask is a honeycomb
of narcotic wasps
and the shaman
gorges on honey
so he fly over cliffs.

Several stone stupas
surround us
and metals
vibrate
indefinably.

A Chinese teapot
of black enamel
and monkeys
over floral collars.

An albino guru
feeds on milk
near the pyres
of the dead.

un ojo
poliédrico
contempla el valle
mientras llueve.

Hay alfombras azules
monocromas
que representan el mar
y las mujeres llevan caracolas
en los brazos.

Las banderas
ondean
al viento
pero todos los tankas antiguos
están rotos.

A lo lejos
los leopardos
y los carneros azules
se ocultan
en la nieve.

On a hill
a poliedric
eye
ponders the valley
while it rains.

There are blue
monochrome carpets
representing the sea
and women wear shells
on their arms.

Flags
flutter
in the wind
but all the ancient tankas
are broken.

In the distance
leopards
and blue sheep
are concealed
in the snow.

La cueva de Milarepa

para Gerald Barry

Montañas nevadas,
ríos torrenciales
y rebaños de yaks.

Entre las piedras,
y al sol,
inmóviles,
las marmotas.

Los peregrinos
en el valle
se arrastran
por los suelos.

Moscas de mantequilla,
cruces gamadas,
gongs,
estandartes
y libros de piedra.

Avida
la mangosta
devora
diamantes
y otras gemas violeta.

Descubro que soy
una campana.

Hic sunt leones.

Milarepa's Cave

for Gerald Barry

Snow-capped mountains,
 torrential rivers
and herds of yaks.

Among the stones,
and in the sunlight,
the marmots,
immobile.

Pilgrims
in the valley
drag themselves
across the ground.

Buttery flies,
swastikas,
gongs,
banners
and books of stone.

Keenly
the mongoose
devours
diamonds
and other violet gems.

I discover I'm
a bell.

Hic sunt leones.

Anochecer en un delta interior de Botswana

El paisaje como capricho
del tiempo.
Troncos retorcidos y muertos,
buitres somnolientos,
y jirafas atentas.

La ciudad infinita de las termitas
rodeada de espinos
y de charcas secas.

Osamentas putrefactas,
manadas de impalas y de cebras,
y al fondo el sol
oculto por el polvo.

El imperio de la ceniza
recubre el amor,
sostenido
tal vez
por la fuerza telúrica del bosque.

Sobre la arena
caen las bayas dulces
que devoran los chacales.

Las ranas
como marimbas
histéricas
encienden el agua.

Dusk Over an Interior Delta in Botswana

The countryside as a caprice
of time.

Contorted and dead tree trunks,
somnolent vultures
and watchful giraffes.

The infinite city of termites
surrounded by thorns
and dried-up ponds.

Putrid carcasses,
herds of impala and zebra,
and the sun in the background
concealed by dust.

The empire of ashes
covers over love,
perhaps
sustained
by the forest's telluric strength.

Sweet berries
fall on the sand
to be gorged by jackals,

Frogs
like hysterical marimbas
set the water on fire.

Tarjeta de visita

para Susy Gómez

Un gato desventrado
y crucificado en el suelo
compite por las moscas
con los pájaros decapitados.

Una semilla de ébano,
amuleto de la memoria,
es un enigma
entre los cráneos de los antílopes.

El hechicero insitente
y profesional
te entrega su tarjeta
al albor de los aligatores:

Eugéne Zopkon
Guérisseur Traditionnel
Marché des Fétiches Akodessewa, BP 61153
Stand 2
Lomé-Togo.

Business Card

for Susy Gómez

A cat gutted open
and crucified on the ground
competes for the flies
with decapitated birds.

An ebony seed,
an amulet of memory,
is an enigma
among the skulls of antelopes.

The persistent
professional witchdoctor
gives you his business card
at the dawn of alligators.

Eugéne Zopkon
Guérisseur Traditionnel
Marché des Fétiches Akodessewa, BP 61153
Stand 2
Lomé-Togo.

Ideogramas sobre barro

El coche levanta una cortina
roja
cuando del polvo surgen
los baobabs
y en el polvo se entierra la laguna.

Las estructuras circulares
y pintadas de los Gurunsi:
celebridad amurallada de Tiébéle.

Los poblados son
receptáculos cúbicos
sin ventanas
de apariencia inmemorial,
con graneros que acaban en sombrillas
de playa.
Unos cilindros de barro
forman ochos
que son las cámaras del amor.

Se detiene el coche
justo cuando acaba
Dugu kamelemba de Oumou Sangare.

El exterior de estas viviendas
es una malla
de símbolos abstractos:
rojos, azules, negros,
o serpientes circundando
los ojos del caimán.

Los sonidos del tam-tam
son redes para la pesca.

Ideogram on Mud

The car raises a red
curtain
when the baobabs
rise from the dust
and the lagoon is buried in dust.

The circular and painted
structures of the Gurunsi:
the walled celebration of Tiébéle.

The villages are cubic
windowless containers
of immemorial appearance.
Their granaries are peaked
with beach hats.
Some mud cylinders
form the figure of eight
and are chambers of love.

The car stops
just when Oumou Sangare's
Dugu kamelemba ends.

The exterior of these dwellings
is a mesh
of abstract symbols:
red, blue, black,
or with snakes winding around
the eyes of the crocodiles.

The sounds of the tam-tam
are fishing nets.

Jeroglíficos hipnóticos
entre gallinas y cabras.

Y en el centro de la fortaleza
—eje de la geometría—,
crece siempre una papaya.

Hypnotic hieroglyphs
among hens and goats.

And in the centre of the fortress
—an axis of geometry—
a papaya tree always grows.

Jubileo de Otumfuo Opoku Ware II

El rey de los Ashanti
jamás
puede tocar el suelo.
es así que se baña
de pie
sobre colmillos de elefante.

Cubre su cuerpo de oro
y de geometrías de algodón
teñidas de colores.

Durante el día ceremonial
los tambores y los instrumentos de viento
flanquean corriendo
las sombrillas rojas, doradas y azules
de los reyes menores,
dibujando la música del cielo
sobre la explanada de tierra
ante el palacio real.

Después, la noche en Kumasi pasa
por el *Old Timer's Club* del Hotel Kingsway,
legendario salón de baile
de los años cincuenta
donde los hombres visten
semidesnudos
ropa tradicional.

Jubilee of Otumfuo Opoku Ware II

The King of Ashanti
can never
touch the ground.
Therefore he bathes
standing
on elephant tusks.

He covers his body with gold
and geometries of dyed
cotton.

During the ceremonial day
drums and wind instruments
in a race outflank
the red, gold and blue parasols
of minor kings,
sketching the sky's music
on the earthen esplanade
before the royal palace.

Later on, the night in Kumasi passes
along the *Old Timer's Club* of the Kingsway Hotel:
a legendary dancehall
of the fifties,
where half-naked men
wear traditional garb.

Bande á part (1967)

Quiero casarme
con Jean-Luc Godard.

Bande á part (1967)

I want to marry
Jean-Luc Godard.

Film

para Mark Healy

Secuencia 1 – Los ojos negros del mariachi. Su pistola enfundada. Llueve torrencialmente sobre la playa. Círculos ascendentes de aves sobre nubarrones enormes.

Secuencia 2 – La bandera arco iris a la entrada de un antro. Música electrónica.

Secuencia 3 – Oscuridad fluorescente. Cuerpos que bailan y miradas que se cruzan (como en *Millenium Mambo* de Hou Hsiao Hsien). Un brazo derriba una hilera de vasos en la barra.

Secuencia 4 – Suena un teléfono y el mariachi despierta. De nuevo sus ojos negros. Un coche cae por un acantilado. Pirámides aztecas inundadas de sangre. El desierto. La sombra de un águila sobre los cactus.

Film

for Mark Healy

Sequence 1. The black eyes of the mariachi. His
holstered gun. It rains torrentially on the beach.
Rising circles of birds
on huge dark clouds.

Sequence 2. The rainbow flag at the entrance of a club.
Electronic music.

Sequence 3. Florescent darkness. Dancing bodies
and mutual gazes (as in Hou Hsiao-Hsien's *Millenium Mambo*).
An arm knocks over a row of glasses on the bar.

Sequence 4. A telephone rings and the mariachi
wakes up. Once more his black eyes. A car goes over a cliff.
Aztec pyramids flooded with blood. The desert. The shadow of an eagle
over the cacti.

La estación de las luciérnagas

Kimonos y abanicos
en las laderas de un monte
rojo.

Enjambres de luces
lentos,
convolutos.
Tentáculos invisibles
y aéreos.

Me deslizo
en llamas
sobre el hielo
y no hay viento alguno
que se acerque
a los árboles inmóviles.

Todo esto lo leo
—Tanizaki—
en una playa vacía
de México.

Cuando el placer es
demasiado intenso
dejo caer el libro
y miro como pescan
los pelícanos.

The Glow-Worm Season

Kimonos and fans
on the slopes of a red
mountain.

Swarms of slow
convoluted
lights.
Invisible and aerial
tentacles.

I slide
in flames
over the ice,
and there is no wind
approaching
the motionless trees.

I am reading all this
—Tanizaki—
on an empty beach
in Mexico.

When the pleasure is
too intense
I let the book fall
and watch how the pelicans
are feeding.

Bachata de Antony Santos debajo de un flamboyán

para Kevin Volans y Pablo Pascual

Sano como un delfín,
en el jardín del hotel
El encuentro poderoso.

Juegan los cuerpos
violentos
bajo el árbol
mientras suena:
"no tengo que ofrecerte
si no es una rosa y un florero
y una copia de un botero
que un día compré en el parque".

La mujer de negro
sin embargo
tiene un aguijón
con el que ataca antes de morir.

Los murciélagos
mientras tanto
son hidroaviones
en la piscina.

Bachata by Antony Santos
Under a Flamboyant Tree

for Kevin Volans and Pablo Pascual

Healthy as a dolphin
in the hotel garden
of *The Powerful Meeting.*

Bodies play
violently
beneath the tree
while there sounds
'I have nothing to give you
but a rose and a vase
and a copy of Botero
I bought one day in the park.'

But the woman in black
has a sting
with which she attacks before dying.

Meanwhile
the bats
are seaplanes
in the swimming pool.

El Cairo

para Isaac Julien

Chilabas y minaretes
entrevistos en el laberinto de niebla.

Después, una colisión
contra los años cincuenta:
el hotel Hilton en el Nilo.

Mezquitas tan puras como palomas limpias
y el recuerdo de la corona del Emperador
de Abisinia.
Soñar Lalibela.

Un figura abandona
la librería *L'Orientaliste:*
Per l'uragano all'apice di furia
Vicino non intensi farsi il sonno.

Atontado por el alcohol,
cae, de noche,
en los brazos del boxeador.

La cama precaria suena
asesinando los muelles
tal tempestad de acero.

Me taladran.

Una vez en el cielo
la palabra engendra el mito.

Cairo

for Isaac Julien

Djeelabas and minarets
glimpsed in a labyrinth of fog.

Afterwards, a crash
against the fifties:
the Hilton Hotel on the Nile.

Mosques as pure immaculate doves
and the memory of the crown of
the Emperor of Abyssinia.
Dreaming Lalibela.

A figure deserts
the L'Orientaliste bookshop:
Per l'uragano all'apice di furia
Vicino non intensi farsi il sonno.

Stunned by alcohol,
he collapses, in the night,
into the arms of the boxer.

The sound of the precarious bed
murdering the springs
in a storm of steel.

I am drilled.

Once in heaven
word engenders myth.

Música para leer a San Juan de la Cruz

Darren Emerson
John Digweed
Sasha
David Seaman
Nick Warren

Morton Feldman

Music to Read Saint John of the Cross

Darren Emerson
John Digweed
Sasha
David Seaman
Nick Warren

Morton Feldman

Abandonando Dakar

for Mercedes Vilardell

Medianoche,
el día de la clausura del Ramadán.

Las calles desiertas del puerto
y los tinglados destartalados.

Las mortecinas luces de la *Ille de la Gorée*
son una pequeña vibración
fantasmagórica,
como la concha amarilla de la *Shell*
que se repite
a la orilla de la carretera.
La misma luz del letrero
con aeroplano
del *Hôtel de la Poste* en Saint-Louis.

Hace unos años,
un asesinato ritual
durante la guerra de Senegal
con Mauritania.
El toque de queda en una ciudad
que deja de recordar a Tintín
para sugerir a Modiano.

La villa de la Embajada:
sillas de Marcel Breuer
sobre pieles de cebra
y un escudo massai.

Una valiosa estatuilla dogón
—la cosmogonía de la serpiente—
desaparece
tras una noche de amor.

Leaving Dakar

for Mercedes Vilardell

Midnight,
last day of Ramadan.

The port's deserted streets
and its rundown platforms.

The fading lights of *Ille de la Gorée*
are a tiny phantasmagoric
vibration
like the yellow *Shell* sign
that is repeated
along the banks of the motorway.
The same light
of the aeroplane lettering
of *Hôtel de la Poste* in Saint-Louis.

Some years ago,
a ritual murder
during the war between Senegal
and Mauritania.
The bugle call in a city
does not recall Tintin
but suggest Modiano.

The Embassy's villa:
chairs of Marcel Breuer
of the zebra hides
and a Massai shield.

A costly Dogon statuette
—the cosmogony of a snake—
vanishes after a night of love.

La realidad,
rumbo a casa,
es otra.
El taxi deja atrás gatos
hambrientos,
hogueras
y montañas de basura.
Infames turbas de nocturnas aves.
Mañana mismo,
por la mañana,
el trabajo y el teléfono.

As I head for home
reality
is something else.
The taxi passes ravenous cats,
fires and mounds of garbage.
Vile densities of nightbirds.
Only tomorrow,
in the morning,
back to work and the telephone.

Chacra Paradiso

Despertar
en Patagonia:
los ñandúes
beben
bajo los álamos.

El perro juega
con un armadillo muerto
mientras los patos y los ibis
revolotean
sobre las charcas.

La mañana es gélida
pero el cielo
está completamente
azul.
Volcanes negros
y glaciares de plata.

Los caballos relinchan
cerca del bosque
petrificado.

Sólo estamos nosotros.
Lejos de las grúas
y de los automóviles furiosos.

El desorden no se impone
y las palabras son muestras del placer.

Chacra Paradiso

To wake up
in Patagonia:
the ostriches
are drinking
under the poplars.

The dog toys
with a dead armadillo
as ducks and ibises
flutter over
ponds.

The morning is freezing
but the sky
is completely blue.
Black volcanoes
and glaciers of silver.

Horses whinny
near the petrified
forest.

We are alone
far away from cranes
and frenetic cars.

Disorder is not imposed
and words are shows of pleasure.

Boulevard Magenta

París es,
por fin,
mi casa
aunque ya estaba escrita
antes de mí.

Los árboles ilusos
enrojecen
y sus ramas hacen sangrar
una columna de nubes.

Boulevard Magenta

Paris is,
finally,
my home
though it was
already written
before me.

The deluded trees
blush
and their branches bleed
a column of clouds.

ENRIQUE JUNCOSA (Palma de Mallorca, 1961) ha publicado en español seis libros de poesía: *Amanecer zulú* (1986), *Pastoral con cebras* (1990), *Libro del océano* (1991, ilustrado por Miquel Barceló), *Peces de colores* (1996), *Las espirales naranja* (2002) y *Bahía de las banderas* (2007).

Juncosa es autor, además, de varios libros de ensayo: *Caravel. Una revista norteamericana de literatura publicada en Mallorca en los años 30* (2000); *Miquel Barceló o el sentimiento del tiempo* (2004), que apareció en francés un año antes; y *Las adicciones. Ensayos sobre arte contemporáneo* (2006), todos ellos publicados en español. También ha publicado, en inglés, *Writers on Howard Hodgkin* [ed.] (2006). Juncosa también ha traducido del inglés al español libros de Djuna Barnes y de Julian Barnes.

Desde 2003, Enrique Juncosa es director del *Irish Museum of Modern Art* en Dublín, desde donde edita la revista *Boulevard Magenta*. Antes fue subdirector del Instituto Valenciano de Arte Moderno, Valencia y del Museo Nacional Centro de Arte Reina Sofía, Madrid.

Juncosa ha comisariado, además, más de treinta exposiciones en diferentes países de Europa y América, entre ellas *Nuevas abstracciones* (Madrid, 1996), *La realidad y el deseo* (Barcelona, 1998), *Big Sur* (Berlin, 2002) y *Order, Desire, Light* (Dublín, 2008), así como numerosas muestras monográficas. De éstas últimas, y entre las más recientes, podemos destacar, Francis Alÿs (2003), Olafur Eliasson (2003), Francesco Clemente (2004), Juan Uslé (2004), Dorothy Cross (2005), Howard Hodgkin (2006), Iran do Espírito Santo (2006), Michael Craig-Martin (2006), Nalini Malani (2007), Miroslaw Balka (2007), James Coleman (2009) y Terry Winters (2009). En 2009, fue comisario de Pabellón Español en la Bienal de Venecia, donde presentó la obra de Miquel Barceló.

ENRIQUE JUNCOSA (b. Palma de Mallorca, 1961) has published six collections of poetry in Spanish: *Amanecer zulú* (1986), *Pastoral con cebras* (1990), *Libro del océano* (1991, illustrated by Miquel Barceló), *Peces de colores* (1996), *Las espirales naranja* (2002) and *Bahía de las banderas* (2007).

Moreover, Juncosa is the author of several books of essays: *Caravel. Una revista americana de literatura publicada en Mallorca en los años 30* (2000); *Miquel Barceló o el sentimiento del tiempo* (2004), which appeared in French the previous year; and *Las adicciones. Ensayos sobre arte contemporáneo* (2006). He has also published in English, *Writers on Howard Hodgkin* (ed.) (2006). In addition, he has translated into Spanish fiction by Djuna Barnes and Julian Barnes.

Since 2003, Enrique Juncosa is the director of the Irish Museum of Modern Art in Dublin, from where he edits the journal *Boulevard Magenta*. Previously he was Deputy Director of the Instituto Valenciano de Arte Moderno, Valencia, and also of the Museo Nacional Centro de Arte Reina Sofía, Madrid.

Among his other achievements, Juncosa has curated more than thirty exhibitions in different countries in Europe and Latin America, among them *Nuevas abstracciones* (Madrid, 1996), *La realidad y el deseo* (Barcelona, 1998), *Big Sur* (Berlin, 2002) and *Order. Desire. Light* (Dublin, 2008), as well as numerous one man shows. Among the most recent of the latter are: Francis Alÿs (2003), Olafur Eliasson (2003), Francesco Clemente (2004), Juan Uslé (2004), Dorothy Cross (2005), Howard Hodgkin (2006), Iran do Espirito Sanro (2006), Michael Craig-Martin (2006), Nalini Malani (2007), Miroslaw Balka (2007), James Coleman (2009) and Terry Winters (2009). In 2009 he was the commissioner for the Spanish Pavilion in the Venice Biennial where he presented the work of Miquel Barceló.

EPILOGUE

This book brings together two books which were published separately in Spain, *Las espirales naranja* (2002) and *Bahía de las banderas* (2007). Readers who have reached this far in the book will be well aware that I have a certain obsession with lists and proper names, of people or places. I am conscious that some of these names may be unknown to readers, thus the reason of the brief glossary that follows. Some other clarifications are also included. I hope some readers will not be offended by the inclusion of glosses on what they already know.

Las espirales naranja / *Orange Spirals*

Self-portrait at 38
Guillaume Apollinaire and Frank O'Hara, French and North American, were, besides being hugely influential poets, great cognoscenti of the art of their respective periods.

The Gold Coast
Acra and Dixcove: cities on the Ghana coast.

Elmina: also on the Ghana coast, is one of numerous fortresses built there by different European nations (Portugal, England, Sweden, Belgium...) for use in the slave trade. Elmina, a gigantic spine-chilling dungeon, was built by the English.

Malcolm Morley: a North American painter born in England, at one stage of his career he used water colours on his frequent travels, which he later used as starting points for his oil paintings.

Car With Cat
Massive Attack: a British musical group whose style has been defined as *hip hop*.

The Gift
"The supreme voice of the world", as Om Koulsum is known is Egypt, is perhaps the best known singer in the Arab world. When she died, thousands attended her funeral in Cairo.

Howard Carter, the British archaeologist who discovered the tomb of Tuttankhamon. His house can be found in front of the ruins of the Temple of Hatshepsut.

Glow-worms for the Axolot
Temaxcal: an esoteric Mayan ritual that consists of spending some time inside a very small promontory, after crawling into it. Inside, the temperature would be extremely high since stones, heated for hours by braziers, were placed in it. The ritual apparently has a purifying function.

Cenote: a subterranean lake. The whole peninsula of Yucatan, where Mayan civilisation developed, is a zone of calcareous rocks where caves and underground waters are common. The axolot is a blind fish that lives in these waters.

Mantra of Love and Ecstasy
This poem consists of a list of names of discotheques in several cities of the world.

The Meridian of Despair
Severo Sarduy: a Cuban poet and novelist, who lived in Paris where he frequented Roland Barthes' circle. His is one of the great names of literature in Spanish at the end of the 20th century.

Novalis: the German romantic poet.

Caspar Friedrich: German romantic painter.

Jorge Guillén: Spanish poet of the generation of Lorca.

Mark Rothko: North American painter.

Lost City
Rainer Werner Fassbinder: German film-maker whose protagonists are sometimes people living in the margins of society.

Happy Together
This is the name of a film directed by the Chinese film-maker Wong Kar-Wai, freely based on a novel by the Argentinian Manuel Puig.

The Opium War in Marang
Marang is on the northeast coast of Malaysia.

Brancusi, the Rumanian sculptor who developed a kind of abstraction starting with organic forms.

The House of Friends
Frederik Kiesler: a very influential North American architect although only one of his buildings is preserved, part of the complex of the Israel Museum of Jerusalem.

James Turrell: a North American artist especially well known for his installations with light.

The Worms

Gabriel Ferrater: a Spanish poet who wrote in Catalan. He published only three books, which were very influential, before he committed suicide.

Library for a Desert Island

Obviously a list of writers. I would, however, like to expand it now with the following names: Roberto Bolaño, Jorge Luis Borges, Robert Byron, Luis de Camões, Elias Canetti, Truman Capote, Philip K. Dick, Seamus Heaney, Yasunari Kawabata, Jack Kerouac, José Carlos Llop, Naguib Mahfouz, Yukio Mishima, Frank O'Hara, Cesare Pavese, Ricardo Piglia, Vikram Seth, James Schuyler, Colm Tóibín and Luis Antonio de Villena.

The Insular Night

Trocadero 162 is the address of the home of the poet José Lezama Lima in Havana; it has now been converted into a museum. Lezama wrote a poem entitled 'La noche insular'. Portraits of various writers, including that of the Cuban poet José Martí, are preserved in his study.

Martin Heidegger: German philosopher.

Terra Lucida

This is a concept of Paradise described in *L'Homme de lumière dans le Soufisme Iranien* by the French writer Henry Corbin.

Bahía de las banderas / Bay of Flags

Fires

Yasunari Kawabata: Japanese novelist.

Juan Navarro Baldeweg: Spanish painter and architect.

Martin Scorsese: North American film-maker.

Marienbad: a spa in which was flimed *Last Year in Marienbad* by the French film-maker, Alain Resnais.

The Museum Rittberg: it houses collections of primitive art and can be found in a neoclassic mansion in Zurich, in which the composer Richard Wagner spent some periods of time.

After Seeing 2046
2046 is a film of the Chinese film-maker Wong Kar-Wai. *Oppiano Licario* is the title of the second novel of José Lezama Lima.

Africa
The delta of the Okavango is a huge interior delta in Botswana where one of the most important natural reserves of Africa can be found.

In the Chinese Pavillion
A bar in Lisbon.

Autobiography
I would like now to add two other names to this list: *Paris nous appartient* by Jacques Rivette and *Luz silenciosa* by Carlos Reygadas.

Bhaktapur
Bhaktapur is a town in the valley of Katmandu in Nepal.

Ideograms On Mud
Tiebelé is a village of the tribe of the Gurunsi, in Burkina Faso. The adobe houses of these villages are profusely decorated with abstract symbols.
     Oumou Sangaré is a popular singer from Mali.

Jubliee of Otumfuo Opoku Ware II
Otumfuo Opoku Ware II was king of the Ashanti in Ghana. He lived in exile in the Seychelles after declaring war on the British Empire. Kumasi is the capital of the country of the Ashanti.

Bande à Part (1967)
This is the name of a film by Jean-Luc Godard, the Swiss film-maker.

Film
Hou Hsiao-Hsien: a Chinese film-maker.

The Glow-worm Season
Junichiro Tanizaki: Japanese novelist.

Bachata by Antony Santos Under a Flamboyant Tree
Antony Santos, a popular singer of the Dominican Republic where the rhythm of the bachata originates; the words in italic are from a song of his.

Cairo
Lalibela is a place in Ethiopia where several medieval Christian churches were built in stone. They are still used.

The verses in Italian are by the poet Giuseppe Ungaretti who lived in Alexandria.

Music to Read Saint John of the Cross
Darren Emerson, John Digweed, Sasha, David Seaman and Nick Warren are disc-jockeys of techno music. Morton Feldman is an avant-garde North American music composer.

Saint John of the Cross was a Spanish mystic poet of the 16th century.

Leaving Dakar
Ille de la Gorée is a small rocky island in front of the city of Dakar in Senegal which served as a basis for the slave trade.

Tintin: a comic character created by the Belgian Hergé.

Patrick Modiano: French novelist whose works often deal with French collaboration during the Second World War.

The Dogons are a people from Mali renowned for their wood carvings.

Chacra Paradiso
Chacra is the Argentinian name given to rather small ranches.

Lightning Source UK Ltd.
Milton Keynes UK
12 December 2009

147418UK00001BA/21/P